No. 326

JOAN
NELSON

with a story by Robert Walser

ROBERT MILLER NEW YORK

FRAU WILKE

by

Robert Walser

ONE DAY, when I was looking for a suitable room, I entered a curious house just outside the city and close to the city tramway, an elegant, oldish, and seemingly rather neglected house, whose exterior had a singularity which at once captivated me.

On the staircase, which I slowly mounted, and which was wide and bright, were smells and sounds as of bygone elegance.

What they call former beauty is extraordinarily attractive to some people. Ruins are rather touching. Before the residues of noble things our pensive, sensitive inward selves involuntarily bow. The remnants of what was once distinguished, refined, and brilliant infuse us with compassion, but simultaneously also with respect. Bygone days and old decrepitude, how enchanting you are!

On the door I read the name "Frau Wilke."

Here I gently and cautiously rang the bell. But when I realized that it was no use ringing, since nobody answered, I knocked, and then somebody approached.

Very guardedly and very slowly somebody opened the door. A gaunt, thin, tall woman stood before me, and asked in a low voice: "What is it you want?"

Her voice had a curiously dry and hoarse sound.

"May I see the room?"

"Yes, of course. Please come in."

The woman led me down a strangely dark corridor to the room, whose appearance immediately charmed and delighted me. Its shape was, as it were, refined and noble, a little narrow perhaps, yet proportionately tall. Not without a sort of irresolution, I asked the price, which was extremely moderate, so I took the room without more ado.

It made me glad to have done this, for a strange state of mind had much afflicted me for some time past, so I was unusually tired and longed to rest. Weary of all groping endeavor, depressed and out of sorts as I was, any acceptable security would have satisfied me, and the peace of a small resting place could not have been other than wholly welcome.

"What are you?" the lady asked.

"A poet!" I replied.

She went away without a word.

An earl, I think, might live here, I said to myself as I carefully examined my new home. This charming room, I said, proceeding with my soliloquy, unquestionably possesses a

No. 331

No. 317

great advantage: it is very remote. It's quiet as a cavern here. Definitely: here I really feel I am concealed. My inmost want seems to have been gratified. The room, as I see it, or think I see it, is, so to speak, half dark. Dark brightness and bright darkness are floating everywhere. That is most commendable. Let's look around! Please don't put yourself out, sir! There's no hurry at all. Take just as much time as you like. The wall-paper seems, in parts, to be hanging in sad, mournful shreds from the wall. So it is! But that is precisely what pleases me, for I do like a certain degree of raggedness and neglect. The shreds can go on hanging; I'll not let them be removed at any price, for I am completely satisfied with them being there. I am much inclined to believe that a baron once lived here. Officers perhaps drank champagne here. The curtain by the window is tall and slender, it looks old and dusty; but being so prettily draped, it betokens good taste and reveals a delicate sensibility. Outside in the garden, close to the window, stands a birch tree. Here in summer the green will come laughing into the room, on the dear gentle branches all sorts of singing birds will gather, for their delight as well as for mine. This distinguished old writing table is wonderful, handed surely down from a past age of great acumen. Probably I shall write essays at it, sketches, studies, little stories, or even long stories, and send these, with urgent requests for quick and friendly publication, to all sorts of stern and highly reputable editors of papers and periodicals like, for example, *The Peking Daily News*, or *Mercure de France*, whence, for sure, prosperity and success must come.

The bed seems to be all right. In this case I will and must dispense with painstaking scrutiny. Then I saw, and here remark, a truly strange and ghostly hatstand, and the mirror there over the basin will tell me faithfully every day how I look. I hope the image it will give me to see will always be a flattering one. The couch is old, consequently pleasant and appropriate. New furniture easily disturbs one, because novelty is always importunate, always obstructs us. A Dutch and a Swiss landscape hang, as I observe to my glad satisfaction, modestly on the wall. Without a doubt, I shall look time and again at these two pictures most attentively. Regarding the air in this chamber, I would nevertheless deem it credible, or rather postulate at once with certitude almost, that for some time here no thought has been given to regular and, it seems, wholly requisite ventilation. I do declare that there is a smell of decay about the place. To inhale stale air provides a certain peculiar pleasure. In any case, I can leave the window open for days and weeks on end; then the right and good will stream into the room.

"You must get up earlier. I cannot allow you to stay in bed so long," Frau Wilke said to me. Beyond this, she did not say much.

No. 308

No. 295

This was because I spent entire days lying in bed.

I was in a bad way. Decrepitude surrounded me. I lay there as if in heaviness of heart; I neither knew nor could find myself any more. All my once lucid and gay thoughts floated in obscure confusion and disarray. My mind lay as if broken in fragments before my grieving eyes. The world of thought and of feeling was jumbled and chaotic. Everything dead, empty, and hopeless to the heart. No soul, no joy any more, and only faintly could I remember that there were times when I was happy and brave, kind and confident, full of faith and joy. The pity of it all! Before and behind me, and all around me, not the slightest prospect any more.

Yet I promised Frau Wilke to get up earlier, and in fact I did then also begin to work hard.

Often I walked in the neighboring forest of fir and pine, whose beauties, wonderful winter solitudes, seemed to protect me from the onset of despair. Ineffably kind voices spoke down to me from the trees: "You must not come to the dark conclusion that everything in the world is hard, false, and wicked. But come often to us; the forest likes you. In its company you will find health and good spirits again, and entertain more lofty and beautiful thoughts."

Into society, that is, where the big world foregathers, I never went. I had no business there, because I had no success. People who have no success with people have no business with people.

Poor Frau Wilke, soon afterwards you died.

Whoever has been poor and lonely himself understands other poor and lonely people all the better. At least we should learn to understand our fellow beings, for we are powerless to stop their misery, their ignominy, their suffering, their weakness, and their death.

One day Frau Wilke whispered, as she stretched out her hand and arm to me: "Hold my hand. It's like ice."

I took her poor, old, thin hand in mine. It was cold as ice.

Frau Wilke crept about her home now like a ghost. Nobody visited her. For days she sat alone in her unheated room.

To be alone: icy, iron terror, foretaste of the grave, forerunner of unpitying death. Oh, whoever has been himself alone can never find another's loneliness strange.

I began to realize that Frau Wilke had nothing to eat. The lady who owned the house, and later took Frau Wilke's rooms, allowing me to stay in mine, brought, of course in pity for her forsaken state, every midday and evening a cup of broth, but not for long, and so Frau Wilke faded away. She lay there, no longer moving: and soon she was taken to the city hospital, where, after three days, she died.

One afternoon soon after her death, I entered her empty

No. 320

No. 314

room, into which the good evening sun was shining, gladdening it with rose-bright, gay and soft colors. There I saw on the bed the things which the poor lady had till recently worn, her dress, her hat, her sunshade and her umbrella, and, on the floor, her small delicate boots. The strange sight of them made me unspeakably sad, and my peculiar state of mind made it seem to me almost that I had died myself, and life in all its fullness, which had often appeared so huge and beautiful, was thin and poor to the point of breaking. All things past, all things vanishing away, were more close to me than ever. For a long time I looked at Frau Wilke's possessions, which now had lost their mistress and lost all purpose, and at the golden room, glorified by the smile of the evening sun, while I stood there motionless, not understanding anything any more. Yet, after standing there dumbly for a time, I was gratified and grew calm. Life took me by the shoulder and its wonderful gaze rested on mine. The world was as living as ever and beautiful as at the most beautiful times. I quietly left the room and went out into the street.

"Frau Wilke" from *The Walk and Other Stories* by Robert Walser, translated by Christopher Middleton. Copyright © John Calder (Publishers) Limited, 1957. Reproduced by permission of Calder Publications Limited, London.

No. 318

No. 310

No. 292

No. 297

No. 301

No. 312

No. 328

No. 286

No. 330

No. 313

No. 325

No. 307

No. 315

No. 304

No. 321

Untitled, (#326), oil on wood, 9 x 6 inches, 22.8 x 15.2cm., 1991

Untitled, (#331), oil and wax on wood, 10 x 10 inches, 25.4 x 25.4cm., 1991

Untitled, (#317), oil and wax on wood, 9 x 6 inches, 22.8 x 15.2cm., 1991

Untitled, (#308), oil on wood, 6 x 12 inches, 15.2 x 30.4cm., 1991

Untitled, (#295), oil and wax on wood, 7 x 7 inches, 17.7 x 17.7cm., 1991

Untitled, (#320), oil, ink and tinted gesso on wood, 12 x 6 inches,
    30.4 x 15.2cm., 1991

Untitled, (#314), gouache on wood, 8 x 8 inches, 20.3 x 20.3cm., 1991

Untitled, (#318), oil on wood, 24 x 12 inches, 60.9 x 30.4cm., 1991

Untitled, (#310), oil and ink on wood, 7 x 7 inches, 17.7 x 17.7cm., 1991

Untitled, (#292), oil on wood, 7 x 7 inches, 17.7 x 17.7cm., 1991

Untitled, (#297), oil on wood, 10 x 10 inches, 25.4 x 25.4cm., 1990

Untitled, (#301), oil and wax on wood, 8 x 8 inches, 20.3 x 20.3cm., 1991

Untitled, (#312), oil and wax on wood, 10 x 10 inches, 25.4 x 25.4cm., 1991

Untitled, (#328), oil and nail enamel on wood, 10 x 10 inches,
    25.4 x 25.4cm., 1991

Untitled, (#286), oil and wax on wood, 12 x 6 inches, 30.4 x 15.2cm., 1990

Untitled, (#330), oil on wood, 14 x 14 inches, 35.5 x 35.5cm., 1991

Untitled, (#313), gouache on wood, 18 x 18 inches, 45.7 x 45.7cm., 1991

Untitled, (#325), oil on wood, 18 x 18 inches, 45.7 x 45.7cm., 1991

Untitled, (#307), oil and gouache on wood, 10 x 10 inches,
    25.4 x 25.4cm., 1991

Untitled, (#315), oil and wax on wood, 6 x 9 inches, 15.2 x 22.8cm., 1991

Untitled, (#304), oil on wood, 7 x 7 inches, 17.7 x 17.7cm., 1991

Untitled, (#321), oil and wax on wood, 10 x 10 inches, 25.4 x 25.4cm., 1991

JOAN NELSON

1958   Born in Torrance, California
1981   Received B.F.A. from Washington University, St. Louis,
         Missouri
1981–82 Awarded Max Beckman Memorial Scholarship, Brooklyn
         Museum School, New York
present Lives and works in New York

SOLO EXHIBITIONS
1985   P.P.O.W. Gallery, New York
1986   P.P.O.W. Gallery, New York
         Michael Kohn Gallery, Los Angeles
1987   Fawbush Gallery, New York
         Michael Kohn Gallery, Los Angeles
1988   Contemporary Arts Museum, Houston, Texas
1989   Robert Miller Gallery, New York
         St. Louis Arts Museum, St. Louis, Missouri, "Currents 39"
1990   Robert Miller Gallery, New York, "Joan Nelson: New
         Paintings"
         Michael Kohn Gallery, Santa Monica, California
1991   Freedman Gallery, Albright College, Reading, Pennsylvania
         Robert Miller Gallery, New York

GROUP EXHIBITIONS
1982   Nature Morte Gallery, New York
1984   P.P.O.W. Gallery, New York
1985   Grace Borgenicht Gallery, New York, "Summer Invitational"

Saidye Bronfman Gallery, Montreal, "East Village at the Center"
Vorpal Gallery, San Francisco, "East Village Artists"
Greenville County Museum of Art, Greenville, South Carolina, "Places"
Jan Baum Gallery, Los Angeles, "Minimal Representation"
Solomon R. Guggenheim Museum, New York, "Exxon Emerging Artists Invitational"
Christminster Gallery, New York
Joe Fawbush Editions, New York, "Works on Paper"

1986   Morris Center, Lafayette College, Easton, Pennsylvania, "Art of the East Village"
Lang O'Hara Gallery, New York, "Small Format"
Delaware Art Museum, Wilmington, Delaware, "NYC: New Work"
American Academy of Arts and Letters, New York, "Art Awards Exhibition"
International Kunstmusee, Zurich, Switzerland, "Forum"
Indianapolis Museum of Art, Indianapolis, Indiana, "Painting and Sculpture Today: 1986"
Lehman College Art Gallery, Bronx, New York, "Landscape in the Age of Anxiety," (travelled to: Cleveland Center for Contemporary Art, Cleveland, Ohio)
Lorence Monk Gallery, New York, "The Manor in the Landscape"
P.P.O.W. Gallery, New York

1987   Curt Marcus Gallery, New York, "On Paper"
Greenberg Gallery, St. Louis, Missouri, "Between Abstraction and Reality"
Michael Kohn Gallery, Los Angeles, California, "The Great Drawing Show"
Fay Gold Gallery, Atlanta, Georgia, "New Impressions"
Jan Turner Gallery, Los Angeles, California, "Joe Fawbush Editions: A Selection"

The Whitney Museum of American Art, Stamford,
Connecticut, "The New Romantic Landscape"
Solomon R. Guggenheim Museum, New York, "Emerging
Artists: Selections from the Exxon Series, 1975–1986"
Kent Fine Art and Curt Marcus Gallery, New York, "Fictions:
A Selection of Pictures from the 18th, 19th, & 20th
Centuries, curated by Douglas Blau

1988   Blum Helman Gallery, New York, "Jack Barth, Michael
Young, Joan Nelson"
Jan Turner Gallery, Los Angeles, California, "Landscape:
Common Ground"
Loughelton Gallery, New York, "Of Another Nature"
Grace Borgenicht Gallery, New York, "Landscape Anthology"
ACA Gallery, New York, "Land"

1989   New York Studio School, New York, "RePresenting
Landscape," curated by Suzaan Boettger
Scott Hanson Gallery, New York, "The Objective World"
Gallery Urban, New York, "Abstraction as Landscape"
Michael Kohn Gallery, Los Angeles, "300 Years of Still Life"
Walker Art Center, Minneapolis, "Landscape Re-Viewed:
Contemporary Reflections on a Traditional Theme"
Whitney at Equitable Center, New York, "Nocturnal Visions
in Contemporary Painting"
Whitney Museum of American Art, New York, "1989
Biennial Exhibition"
Betsy Rosenfield Gallery, Chicago, "Landscape"
Ruth Siegel Gallery Ltd., New York, "Landscape: A
Travelogue Painted from Memory, Imagination or Reality"
Kunetsky Most Exhibition Hall, Moscow, USSR, "Painting
Beyond The Death of Painting," (American Imagistic and
Abstract Work) in association with USSR Artists Union and
New York Artists in Moscow

Richard Green Gallery, Los Angeles, California, "Landscape Constructions," curated by Suzaan Boettger

Fuller Gross Gallery, Los Angeles, "Topology"

American Academy of Arts and Letters, New York, "41st Annual Purchase Exhibition"

1989–91   Art Gallery of Western Australia, Perth, Australia, "Romance and Irony in Recent American Art," (originating institution), opened at National Art Gallery, Wellington, New Zealand, (travelled to: Art Gallery of Western Australia, Perth; Auckland City Art Gallery, New Zealand; Tampa Museum of Art, Florida; Parrish Art Museum, Southampton, New York

1990   Museum of Art, Rhode Island School of Design, Providence, Rhode Island, "Terra Incognita: New Directions in Contemporary Landscape"

The University Art Galleries, Wright State University, Dayton, Ohio, "Joan Nelson/Gary Stephan Landscapes"

Zoe Gallery, Boston, "This Land is Our Land"

Solo Press/Solo Gallery, New York, "Writ in Water"

Lehman College Art Gallery, Bronx, New York, "Botanica: The Secret Life of Flowers"

A/D, New York, "The Garden," Spring-Fall, changing installation

Wiener Festwochen, Vienna, Austria, "Von der Natur in Der Kunst"

Virginia Museum of Fine Arts, Richmond, "Harmony & Discord"

Witte de With, Rotterdam, The Netherlands, "The Ten Artists I was Thinking of on May 3, 1990 at 7:00 o'clock," curated by Jiri Georg Dokoupil

American Academy and Institute of Arts and Letters, New York, "42nd Annual Academy—Institute Purchase Exhibition"

	Galeria Leyendecker, Santa Cruz de Tenerife, Canary Islands, Spain, "Third International Exhibition"
1991	New Britain Museum of American Art, New Britain, Connecticut, "1991 Invitational"
	Tibor de Nagy Gallery, New York, "Working with Wax: Ten Contemporary Artists"
	Southeastern Center for Contemporary Art, Winston-Salem, North Carolina, "The Eternal Landscape"
	Forum Gallery, New York, "Summer"
	Galerie Pfefferle, Munich, "A Dialogue of Images—Recent German and American Painting"
	Michael Kohn Gallery, Santa Monica, California, "Joan Nelson, Kevin Lamon, Vincent Shrine"
1991–92	The Miyagi Museum of Art, Miyagi, Japan, "American Realism & Figurative Art: 1952–1990;" (organized by John Arthur), (travelled to: Sogo Museum of Art; The Tokushima Modern Art Museum; The Museum of Modern Art, Shiga; Kochi Prefectural Museum of Folk Art)
	Modern Art Museum of Fort Worth, Texas, "Refiguring Nature"
1992	Seville World Expo '92, United States Pavilion, "New Viewpoints: Contemporary Paintings by Distinguished American Women Artists"

PUBLIC COLLECTIONS

Museum of Modern Art, New York

Solomon R. Guggenheim Museum, New York

Toledo Museum of Art, Toledo, Ohio

Archer M. Huntington Art Gallery, University of Texas at Austin

Los Angeles County Museum of Art

Minneapolis Museum of Art

BOOKS AND CATALOGUES

1985

New Horizons in American Art, (exhibition catalogue), essay by Lisa
    Dennison, New York: Exxon National Exhibition, Solomon R.
    Guggenheim Museum.

1987

The New Romantic Landscape, (exhibition catalogue), essay by Chantal
    Combes, Stamford: Whitney Museum of American Art.
Emerging Artists 1978–1986: Selections From The Exxon Series, essay by Diane
    Waldman, New York: Solomon R. Guggenheim Museum.

1988

Beckett, Wendy, Contemporary Women Artists, Oxford: Phaidon.
Ranta, Rachel. (essay for brochure), Joan Nelson Paintings, Houston, Texas:
    Contemporary Arts Museum.

1989

Armstrong, Richard and Richard Marshall. 1989 Biennial Exhibition, (ex-
    hibition catalogue), New York: Whitney Museum of American Art.
_____. Joan Nelson/Currents 39, (brochure), St. Louis, Missouri: The Saint
    Louis Art Museum.
Gratchos, Louis with John Stringer and Richard Martin. Romance and Irony
    in Recent American Art, (exhibition catalogue), Perth: Art Gallery of
    Western Australia.
Rosenberg, Barry A. Joan Nelson/Gary Stephen Landscapes, (exhibition cata-
    logue), Dayton, Ohio: The University Art Galleries at Wright State
    University.

1990

_____. Von der Natur in Der Kunst, (exhibition catalogue), Vienna, Austria:
    Wiener Festwochen.

Freeman, Phyllis with Mark Greenberg, Eric Himmel, Andras Landshoff et. al. *New Art*, New York: Harry N. Abrams, Inc., p. 146–147.

Kuspit, Donald. *Joan Nelson*, (exhibition catalogue), New York: Robert Miller Gallery.

_____. *Harmony & Discord: American Landscape Painting Today*, Richmond: Virginia Museum of Fine Arts.

Dokoupil, Jiri Georg. *Die zehn Kunstler an die ich am 3. Mai 1990 um 19.00 Uhr gedacht habe.* (exhibition catalogue), Rotterdam: Witte de With.

La Motta, Janice. *1991 Invitational,* (exhibition catalogue), New Britain, Connecticut: New Britain Museum of American Art.

Kuspit, Donald and Paul Groot. *Regreso al Futuro III Exposicion Internacional.* (exhibition catalogue). Las Palmas de Gran Canaria: Casa de la Cultura, Santa Cruz de Tenerife, Centro de arte La Regenta.

1991

Schifferman, Janice McGill. *Joan Nelson* (pamphlet to accompany exhibition). Reading, Pennsylvania: Freedman Gallery, Albright College.

Kuspit, Donald. *A Dialogue of Images Zeitgenössische Amerikanische und Deutsche Malerei.* (exhibition catalogue). Munich: Galerie Pfefferle.

1992

Betti, Claudia and Teel Sale. *Drawing: A Contemporary Approach*. Texas: Holt, Rinehart and Winston, Inc.

PERIODICALS
1982

Moufarrege, Nicolas. "Group Show; Nature Morte," *Arts*, vol. 57, no. 2, October, p. 19.

1985

Raynor, Vivien. "Joan Nelson," (at P.P.O.W. Gallery, New York), *The New York Times*, February 8, p. C32.

Indiana, Gary. "Invitational Exhibition," *The Village Voice*, June 11, p. 74.

"An American Landscape," *Bomb*, (reproduction of UNTITLED 1984),
  Winter issue, vol. XI, p. 69.

1986

Brenson, Michael. "Joan Nelson," (at P.P.O.W. Gallery, New York), *The New York Times*, February 28, p. C25.

Sturtivant, Alfred. "Hearts and Minds," *New York Native*, no. 152, March 17.

Larson, Kay. "New Faces of '86," *New York*, vol. 19, no. 12, March 24, 1986, pp. 84–85.

Goldberg, Shellie R. "Joan Nelson; P.P.O.W.," *Art News*, vol. 85, no. 5, May 1986, pp. 132–133.

McKenna, Kristine. review of exhibition at Michael Kohn Gallery, Los Angeles, *Los Angeles Times*, June 13, part VI, p. 17.

Indiana, Gary. "The Manor in the Landscape," *The Village Voice*, December 16, 1986, p. 119.

Laurence, Michael. "Joan Nelson," *West Hollywood Paper*, vol. 1, no. 46, July 3–10.

1987

Brenson, Michael. "Are the Whitney's Satellites Out of Orbit?," *The New York Times*, August 9, section 2, pp. 31–32.

Brenson, Michael. "Joan Nelson; Fawbush Gallery," *The New York Times*, October 2, p. C27.

"Album: Joan Nelson," *Arts*, vol. 62, no. 2, October, pp. 106–107.

Cohrs, Timothy. "Joan Nelson; Fawbush Gallery," *Arts*, vol. 62, no. 3, November, p. 111.

Loughery, John. "The New Romantic Landscape," *Arts*, vol. 62, no. 3, November, p. 107.

Curtis, Cathy. "Joan Nelson" (at Michael Kohn Gallery, Los Angeles), *Los Angeles Times*, December 18, part VI, p. 22.

Arts, (illustration used), September, pp. 106–107.

1988

Haus, Mary Ellen. "The Unnatural Landscape," *Artnews*, vol. 87, no. 1, January, pp. 128–132.

Kuspit, Donald. "Joan Nelson; Fawbush Gallery," *Artforum*, vol. 26, no. 5, January, pp. 113–114.

Boettger, Suzaan. "Joan Nelson at Fawbush," *Arts*, vol. 76, no. 2, February, pp. 141 - 142.

Mahoney, Robert. review of Blum Helman summer show, "Jack Barth, Joan Nelson, Michael Young," *Arts*, October, p. 101.

McCombie, Mel. "Nature Confronted With Artifice," *Artweek*, May 14, (Houston, Texas publication), vol. 19, no. 19, p. 7.

Johnson, Patricia C. "The Dichotomy of Big, Small," *Houston Chronicle*, May 1, p. 16.

Chadwick, Susan. "Artist Paints Revolutionary View of the World," *The Houston Post*, Sunday, May 8, p. 4F.

Loughery, John. "Landscape Painting in the Eighties: April Gornik, Ellen Phelan and Joan Nelson," *Arts*, May, p. 44–48.

1989

Zimmer, William. "Eva Hesse/Joan Nelson," *Artnews*, April, p. 198 & 199.

Johnson, Ken. "Joan Nelson at Robert Miller," *Art in America*, March, p. 144.

Pryor, Kelly. "Back to Nature," *Avenue*, February, p. 128–137.

Glueck, Grace. "The New Romantics Paint The Past," *The New York Times*, ("The New Season"—magazine supplement), September 10, p. 45, 63 & 64.

Smith, Roberta. "A Shift in Perspective," *Vogue*, May, p. 230, 232, 234.

Degener, Patricia. "Nelson's Landscapes Hark Back to Old Masters," *St. Louis Post-Dispatch*, Sunday, March 12, p. 4C.

Galligan, Gregory. "Rescripting the Sublime," *Art International*, Summer, pp. 56-59.

Kimmelman, Michael. "So Sad, So Pastoral, So End of the Century," *The New York Times*, October 20, p. C27.

_____. "Transforming the Landscape," *Bijutso Techo*, 1989/12, pp. 26, 27, 29, 72.

Brenson, Michael. "Straightened Landscapes of a Post-Modern Era," *The New York Times*, January 13, p. C32.

_____. *The Paris Review*, cover illustration, vol. 31, no. 113, Winter II,

1990

Larson, Kay. "Back to Nature," *New York*, April 2, vol. 23, no. 13, p. 63.

Curtis, Cathy. "Old Master Landscapes," *The Los Angeles Times*, March 16, section F, p. 22.

Kuspit, Donald. "Joan Nelson: A Strategy of Partial Quotation," (excerpt from catalogue), *Art/World*, vol. 14, no. 4, 5, 6, February, March, April.

Smith, Roberta, "Joan Nelson," *The New York Times*, March 30, p. C24.

Kernan, Michael. "A New Generation of Artists Ponder Nature's Prospects," *Smithsonian*, April, vol. 21, no. 1, pp. 104–111.

Boodro, Michael. "Joan Nelson Second Nature," *Artnews*, September, vol. 89, no. 7, pp. 142–147 and cover.

1991

Edelman, Robert G. "Paysage recyclé: le paysage dans la peinture américaine contemporaine," *Art press*, March, n. 156, pp. 22-29.

Honda, Hiromi. "Joan Nelson," *Hangwa Geijutsu*, n. 71, pp. 156–158.

Smith, Roberta. "On Long Island, Photos, Portraits, Pollock and Stereotyping," *The New York Times*, August 9, p. C22.

_____. "Romance and Irony," *Arts Review*, June 11-July 8, no pg. number.

Lipson, Karin. "Modern Romantic Vision," *New York Newsday*, June 28, section II.

Braff, Phyllis. "Exhibition Is Window On Society," *The New York Times*, July 28, LI section.

_____. "Romance and Irony in Recent American Art/The Parrish Art Museum," *Journal of the Print World*, Summer, p. 47.

Hay, R. Couri. "High Society," *Hamptons*, June 21, p. 40.

Slivka, Rose C.S. "From the Studio," *The East Hampton Star*, July 11, p. B11.

This book accompanies an exhibition
of paintings by Joan Nelson
at the Robert Miller Gallery New York
November 19 to December 28, 1991

Edited and designed by John Cheim
Production by Ink, Inc.
Printed by The Stinehour Press
ISBN #0-944-680-38-0